THE GRAMMAR SCHOOL QUESTION

A REVIEW OF RESEARCH ON COMPREHENSIVE AND SELECTIVE EDUCATION

D1313183

Institute of Education

UNIVERSITY OF LONDON

The Grammar School Question

A review of research on comprehensive and selective education

DAVID CROOK
SALLY POWER
GEOFF WHITTY

First published in 1999 by the
Institute of Education University of London,
20 Bedford Way, London WC1H 0AL
Tel: 020 7612 6000 Fax: 020 7612 6126

Pursuing Excellence in Education

British Library Cataloguing in Publication Data:
a catalogue record for this publication is available
from the British Library

ISBN 0 85473 608 5

Produced in Great Britain by
Reprographic Services
Institute of Education University of London

Printed by Formara Limited
16 The Candlemakers, Temple Farm Industrial
Estate, Southend on Sea, Essex SS2 5RX

I1/0007-PEP No7-0999

CONTENTS

ACKNOWLEDGEMENTS

This review substantially draws upon a report by the authors for Medway Council. We are grateful to Richard Bolsin, Director of Education for Medway Council, for sponsoring the original work.

We would also like to thank members of Medway Council's Education Department and Professor Richard Aldrich for their helpful comments on earlier drafts.

ABBREVIATIONS

CASE   Campaign for State Education

CSE   Certificate of Secondary Education

CTC   City Technology College

DES   Department of Education and Science

DFE   Department for Education

DfEE   Department for Education and Employment

EBRS   Electoral Reform Ballot Services

GCSE   General Certificate of Secondary Education

GM   Grant Maintained

ILEA   Inner London Education Authority

LEA   Local Education Authority

LMS   Local Management of Schools

NCB   National Children's Bureau

NCDS   National Child Development Study

NCES   National Council for Educational Standards

NFER   National Foundation for Educational Research

NGSA   National Grammar Schools Association

NUT   National Union of Teachers

Ofsted Office for Standards in Education

STEP   Stop the Eleven Plus

TES   Times Educational Supplement

FOREWORD

The Grammar School Question documents the legislative and historical changes that have affected selective education over the last thirty years and endeavours to make sense of the various attempts to compare grammar, secondary modern and comprehensive school performances. Its three authors – an educational historian, a social policy analyst and an educational sociologist – lay out the evidence with admirable clarity, exposing its weaknesses and noting its claims. They offer few personal views and make no policy proposals. Their work is essential background reading for all those engaged in contemporary debates on the future of schooling: the greater agreement over the facts, the easier it will be to focus on contrasting values and different aspirations. The argument over the future of a relatively small number of schools has a greater significance than might at first be assumed. It provides an opportunity to focus on one of the critical questions facing our society: how best to promote the achievement and personal development of all our pupils.

PETER MORTIMORE
Director, Institute of Education

1
Introduction

The election of the new Labour government in May 1997 brought the question of the future of grammar schools back into the policy arena. In an attempt to reconcile the competing claims for school choice and educational equity, Sections 104 to 108 of the School Standards and Framework Act (1998) made it possible for parents to decide the future of the remaining state grammar schools in England by means of local ballots. This policy, designed to give local parents the final say concerning the continuance of selection, is highly controversial. It has attracted criticism from a wide range of commentators and interest groups.

Surrounding the current debates is a strong sense of *déjà vu*. Lady Thatcher has recalled that, during the early 1970s when she was Secretary of State for Education and Science, 'people like me' who had

1

been to 'good grammar schools' were 'strongly opposed to their destruction' (Thatcher, 1995:157). Those preservationist sentiments have been echoed recently in the leading headline of one national newspaper on the morning following parliamentary approval of the ballot regulations. 'Death by ballot for top schools', screamed the *Daily Telegraph* (18 November 1998).

Perhaps it is not surprising that grammar schools evoke such strong passions:[1] some of the threatened grammar schools are among the best performing state schools in the country according to the annual published tables of examination performance at GCSE and 'A' level, and are often seen as the last bastions of excellence in a sea of mediocrity. When Anthony Crosland's famous Circular 10/65 (discussed in section two below) was published in 1965, there were well over 1,000 British grammar schools. As from September 1999,[2] only 164 such schools remain in the state system, all in England.

It is against this background that the future of the last remaining state grammar schools is being debated. In addition to the central question of the relative strengths and weaknesses of comprehensive and selective systems of education, which is examined later in this review, controversies have focused on lack of consistency in selection processes and the nature of the proposed ballots.

Where grammar schools continue to operate in England, the '11-plus' admissions process usually involves Year 6 primary pupils sitting one or more tests, sometimes purchased from bodies such as the National Foundation for Educational Research (NFER). There may also be more qualitative elements involved in selection. For example, information from the child's primary school may also be used. During the middle decades of the twentieth century the process of 11-plus testing was closely scrutinized and frequently criticized. By contrast in recent years there has been very little public discussion of the selection procedures operated by those local education authorities (LEAs) which retained grammar schools, or by grammar schools which administer their own testing arrangements. At the beginning of 1999, however, a well publicized Ofsted report questioned the fairness of the academic selection process in Kent, a country in which 33 grammar schools are located, some 20 per cent of the national total. Fifteen of these schools are LEA grammars, each of which uses a single 11-plus exam. The remaining 18 Kent grammar schools are grant-maintained (GM), each having its own control over admissions and using at least three different 11-plus examinations. The diversity of these selective procedures, together with the fact that many Kent grammar school places are filled on appeal to panels of head teachers without the means to moderate decisions made in different parts of the county, lay at the heart of the inspectors' concerns. Those campaigning for an end to selective schools were naturally delighted by these findings (*The Guardian*, 13 January 1999).

Lack of coherence within secondary provision is also evident in the patchy distribution of the remaining grammar schools. While some areas, such as Kent, are almost completely selective, some other authorities may have just one grammar school within their boundaries. This variability has implications for the ballots that will be held. The Education (Grammar School Ballots) Regulations of 1998 envisage three contexts in which ballots could be held:

- a relevant area containing grammar schools
- a group of grammar schools
- a stand alone grammar school

The 164 grammar schools listed in Appendix A are categorized according to the type of ballot that would apply in each instance. In the cases of schools listed under Surrey and Sutton the type of ballot is subject to the Secretary of State's ruling.

The Department for Education and Employment (DfEE) procedures relating to grammar school ballots were subject to two consultation processes. In the wake of the Labour Party's 1997 general election victory an initial consultation letter was sent to the schools identified at that time by the DfEE as being grammar schools. The letter was also sent to 37 LEAs which at that time had – or from April 1998 were due to have – grammar schools in their areas. Many LEAs circulated the letter to schools in their area. According to the then School Standards Minister, Stephen Byers, some 1,100 responses were received (*Hansard*, 1997). Draft regulations were then drawn up and issued for consultation on 3 June, before the Committee stage of the Bill. These were sent to all grammar schools, LEAs and certain other organizations. Some 322 responses were received, copies of which were placed in the House of Commons Library.

The School Standards and Framework Act (1998) subsequently laid down a specific distinction between the electorate for two sorts of ballot. In an 'area ballot', all the parents resident in the area (excluding those whose children are all 16 years or older), regardless of whether their children are attending any particular type of school, together with parents from outside the area who send their children to maintained schools in the area, will be eligible to petition and vote. By contrast, in 'feeder school ballots', parents of children at primary schools which have sent five children to a 'stand alone' grammar school, or to any of the schools in a group over a period of three years, will be able to petition and vote.

Electoral Reform Ballot Services (ERBS), formerly the Electoral Reform Society, has been chosen by DfEE tender to administer the ballots. ERBS will act as the 'designated body' in accordance with the terms of the Act. A ballot can be triggered by a petition submitted by 20 per cent of eligible parents on relevant school lists held by ERBS. ERBS is not required to start establishing the threshold until requested to do so by ten people, rather than one as stated in the original draft regulations. The DfEE will reimburse the costs incurred by ERBS in providing these services. In January 1999 it was reported that ERBS was preparing electoral lists in Barnet and Ripon, having been contacted by the requisite number of parents (*Daily Telegraph*, 16 January 1999). Similar requests followed from groups of parents from Birmingham and Kingston-upon-Thames, but no petitions were sent to EBRS before the end of the 1998-99 school year. At the time of completing this report (August 1999), therefore, no ballots have been scheduled. It seems very probable, however, that a number of petitions will be presented at the beginning of the year 1999-2000. The regulations state that petitions can run for up to one school year, but cannot continue into a second school year. Certain specified information is to be entered on petitions so that EBRS can check that signatures are eligible.

The meaning of 'eligible parent' is set out in Part I, Paragraph 4 of Statutory Instrument 1998 No. 2876, the Education (Grammar School Ballots) Regulations 1998. The relevant wording may also be found in Appendix B of this report. The order came into force on 3 December 1998.

Grammar school ballots will be secret and conducted by post. They will require parents to respond to the following question:

Are you in favour of all the schools listed introducing admission arrangements which admit children of all abilities?

Place a cross (X) in the box of your choice.

YES ☐   NO ☐

In the case of a feeder school ballot, the stand-alone grammar school's name will be inserted into the question. Otherwise, the ballot paper will list the schools that are involved.

The choice of wording for the ballots has attracted criticism from both the supporters and opponents of grammar schools. Supporters have claimed that the question is 'rigged'. For instance, the word 'grammar school' is not used on the ballot form, leading Damian Green, the Conservative education spokesperson, to allege that the Government is 'trying to push parents into voting yes rather than no' (quoted in *Guardian*, 18 November 1998). As Jack Straw, then the Shadow Education Secretary, pointed out in 1992:

> If you ask people if they believe in grammar schools, they will say yes. If you ask them whether 80 per cent of children should be condemned to secondary modern schools, they will say no... The truth about selection is that it enjoys considerable support among parents whose children pass the 11-plus, and considerable opposition among those whose children fail it (quoted in *Daily Telegraph*, 26 February 1992).

The question of eligibility to petition and vote in the ballots has also proved politically contentious. In their draft form the regulations attracted criticism from both Labour and Conservative politicians (see, for example, *Hansard*, 1998). Four areas of particular controversy may be identified:

a)   parents whose youngest children are in the sixth form will not be eligible to petition or vote in either type of ballot, because the arrangements do not apply to post-16 selective admission. This is in recognition of the fact that all the remaining English grammar schools have sixth forms, but some secondary modern and comprehensive schools do not.

b)   in relation to feeder school ballots, parents whose children currently attend a grammar school will not have a vote on the future status of that school. According to Baroness Blackstone, the Education Minister, allowing this group of parents a vote would strengthen the case for enfranchizing parents of pupils at all secondary schools in the area (*Hansard*, 1998).

c)   also in relation to feeder school ballots, some primary schools which might claim to have a legitimate interest in the outcome of ballots may be too small to send the minimum of five pupils to the grammar school during a three-year period.

d) if a ballot result indicates support for a grammar school or grammar schools within an LEA there remains the possibility of another ballot after five years. To some, this is seen as potentially disruptive.

Awareness of possible grammar school ballots has been raised by the activities of the Campaign for State Education (CASE). CASE launched its national 'Say No to Selection' campaign at the Institute of Education, University of London on 24 October 1998, with contributions from a range of speakers, including Lord Hattersley, Michael Mansfield QC and the pro-comprehensive Dimitri Coryton of the Conservative Education Association. Advice and guidance regarding the presentation of petitions is being offered to parents by CASE by means of information packs and via that organization's web site http://www.mandolin.demon.co.uk/case.html. The tactics of preservationist groups are harder to discern. In Kent and Medway, the grammar schools have been championed by a pressure group led by Eric Hammond, the former leader of the electricians' union. Parent-teacher associations (PTAs) of grammar schools are likely to mount vigorous defences. Some of the PTAs in question have charitable status, which has implications for the conduct of their campaigns. While these bodies may, according to Charity Commission regulations, legitimately engage in activities with a political dimension, the information they disseminate may not be party political in its nature (*Daily Telegraph*, 12 February 1999). At a national level, the National Grammar Schools Association (NGSA) has maintained a surprisingly low profile since late 1998. The explanation for this, according to Catherine Bennett, a *Guardian* columnist, is that the NGSA has 'decided that making a fuss about ballots will simply trigger more of them' (*The Guardian*, 11 February 1999).

Whether or not there are widespread ballots, and whether or not any grammar schools are actually redesignated as comprehensives, there is likely to be intense debate over the coming months – if not years.

The immediate purpose of this publication is to inform any discussions that may arise in relation to these grammar school ballots. However, in view of the enduring issue of differentiation within the English education system, it is hoped that the review will also be of value to those with more general interests.

The remainder of this report is divided into three main sections. Section two provides a brief historical overview of the development of English secondary education with particular reference to dimensions of selective and comprehensive secondary schooling. The third section reviews a number of research studies and other reports relating to selective and comprehensive education published during the past 30 years. In conclusion, some of the implications of ending or retaining selection are discussed.

Notes

1. The depth of feeling over selective education is evident in the recent report that a disagreement between Jeremy Corbyn MP and his wife over whether their eldest son should go to Queen Elizabeth's Boys' Grammar School, Barnet rather than to their local secondary school, Holloway Comprehensive, led to the break up of their marriage (*Daily Telegraph*, 13 May 1999).

2. Prior to this there were 166, but two former Bristol grammar schools decided to admit a comprehensive Year 7 intake from September 1999.

2
Historical overview

THE DEVELOPMENT OF EARLY STATE SECONDARY EDUCATION

Just as continental education systems of the nineteenth century were segmented, defining an academic and a social scale (Ringer, 1979), the people of Victorian England 'knew that elementary education was for working-class children and that grammar schools were for middle-class children' (Silver and Silver, 1991:167). Following legislation of 1902, LEA-maintained grammar schools (for girls, as well as boys) were eventually established in almost every major centre of population, where (together with the endowed grammar schools) they were seen both as the symbols of educational advance and the guardians of cultural excellence. For the working-class child, the acquisition of a highly competitive grammar school scholarship or free place represented a considerable success, although families sometimes experienced difficulties in meeting the costs of a uniform and books, and in some instances fees, as well as adjusting to the loss of assumed juvenile earnings. From 1917, grammar school courses were linked to School Certificate accreditation, strengthening links with the universities, and reinforcing the widely held perception that a grammar school education could open doors that would otherwise remain firmly shut. In short, grammar schools provided an academic education for a minority destined for white-collar work or for university, followed by a professional career. The majority of children, by contrast, received only a basic education in an elementary school, occasionally followed by a short period in a lower status secondary institution.

It was not until after the end of the Second World War that post-elementary or secondary education ceased to be a minority privilege, and instead became a right for all children. The process that led to 'secondary education for all' can be seen as part of a twentieth-century international movement that has sought to weaken the influence of social class upon educational access and achievement. Consistent with research findings from several other countries (Shavit and Blossfeld, 1993), however, significant educational inequalities were to persist. One important study has suggested that, while British working-class children increased their prospects of transferring to a grammar school during the inter-war years, the advantages enjoyed by children of a higher social status did not diminish (Halsey, Heath and Ridge, 1980:62-65).

The educational settlement ushered in by the 1944 Education Act did not seek to challenge the cultural *status quo*, and most of the post-war development plans produced by LEAs contemplated differentiated secondary schooling. The orthodoxy that intelligence was measurable by psychometric tests, offering 'a neutral means of assessing the aptitudes of children from deprived backgrounds and of allocating them to appropriate schools' (Thane, 1982:204) had, by this time, dominated a generation of educational thinking. A tripartite arrangement of secondary grammar, technical and modern schools was widely envisaged, but it was *bipartism* which was to prevail throughout most of the British Isles during the 1950s and 1960s. Properly equipped technical schools proved too expensive for more than a handful of LEAs and, in any case, there were many reservations about identifying the 'technical aptitudes' of a child aged ten-and-a-half (Kerckhoff, Fogelman, Crook and Reeder, 1996:136). The absence of technical schools further militated against the realization of 'parity of esteem' between all state secondary schools. Predictably, parental aspirations favoured the higher status grammar schools, in spite of, or perhaps because of, the fact that, on average, 75 per cent of 11 to 15 year-olds were allocated to secondary modern schools which were merely 'an extension of the elementary school tradition' (Lawton, 1975:3).

DEMANDS FOR COMPREHENSIVE SECONDARY SCHOOLING

Although the implementation of the 1944 settlement was presided over by the same Labour government that created the modern welfare state, egalitarian educational thinking is hard to detect (Judge, 1984:68; Fenwick, 1976:58). A British multilateral (or comprehensive) school lobby, consisting of some socialist politicians and union officials, is identifiable from the 1920s, but few arguments were voiced in favour of radical change. Grammar schools, a number of which enjoyed reputations for excellence dating back to the sixteenth century, had been successful in producing a formidable generation of Labour politicians at both the national and local levels. Moreover, they aroused sentiments of civic pride that tended to push aside considerations of the less-satisfactory secondary modern experience to which most children were exposed. By contrast, multilateral schools were untried, and their anticipated size – to accommodate in excess of 1,000 pupils – was a cause of concern. Some critics viewed their possible introduction as a threat to the social order; for example, writing in the *Times Educational Supplement* (TES) on 1 February 1947, Eric James, High Master of Manchester Grammar School, expressed the fear that they might precipitate 'grave social, educational and cultural evils which may well be a national disaster' (quoted in Rubinstein and Simon, 1969:37). Despite its reputation as a landmark piece of twentieth-century social legislation (Barber, 1994), statistical research based on four English and Welsh male birth cohorts has reported 'no basis' to believe that the 1944 Education Act reduced the effects of socio-economic status on educational attainment' (Kerckhoff and Trott, 1993:149).

The secondary modern school curriculum originally had a strong vocational bias, while the grammar schools exercized a near-monopoly over the teaching of classical and modern foreign languages, and normally possessed the best resources to emphasize pupil accomplishments in art, literature and music. From the late 1950s, the secondary modern curriculum began to imitate that of the grammar schools, but opportunities for obtaining public examination qualifications in secondary moderns remained restricted. Whether or not it was well-founded, the perception that a grammar school education conferred the requisite social and cultural advantages for personal and career advancement remained strong.

In the late 1950s, a handful of diverse English and Welsh LEAs began to establish 'experimental' comprehensive schools. By 1963 a clear trend had developed, partly driven by mounting concerns that the rationale for and methods of psychometric testing were flawed (Vernon, 1957; Yates and Pidgeon, 1957). Originally, support for comprehensive schools was mostly to be found among individuals and groups associated with the Labour movement, but by the early 1960s it had become more widespread. In some localities Conservatives were content to support the removal of the 11-plus in order to facilitate the development of carefully planned comprehensive schemes (Crook, 1993). Others revealed more audacious agendas, hailing comprehensive education as a panacea that might forge a less-divided society and achieve cultural unification (Halsey, 1965:13).

CIRCULARS 10/65 AND 10/70

In July 1965, the Labour government sought further to accelerate the drive towards comprehensive education by issuing a non-statutory circular, Circular 10/65 (DES, 1965). In keeping with the tradition of de-centralized policy-making, English and Welsh LEAs were only *requested* to provide comprehensive plans and, moreover, six possible reorganization models were offered for their consideration. Grammar schools, and secondary moderns too, each had a sense of identity which, though not universally admired, was at least understood. The essential character of a comprehensive school proved more difficult to define. The 'experimental' comprehensives of the late 1950s, in such places as London, Coventry and Bristol, had overwhelmingly been purpose-built institutions, catering for the full 11 to 18 age range and serving areas of new housing. Their establishment had not necessitated school closures, and, while some of them had introduced innovative curricular features (see, for example, London County Council, 1961), their pupil intakes were often similar to secondary modern schools. By the mid-1960s, however, the comprehensive education movement could only proceed if LEAs were willing to abandon the '11-plus' grammar school entrance examination and close, merge or redesignate their existing selective institutions. A lead had been provided by such LEAs as Anglesey, Bradford, Croydon, Leicestershire and the West Riding of Yorkshire. The three latter LEAs each developed non-selective tiered patterns of secondary education that departed from the original conception of a very large comprehensive school.

Labour's policy accepted that diversity was the price to be paid for rapid change. The Department of Education and Science (DES) also accepted a number of secondary reorganization plans that sought only to soften selection, rather than remove it altogether. Though sometimes described as 'interim' solutions, a number of approved LEA proposals contemplated the preservation of at least one grammar school which could 'cream' the most academically able children of the district. Such arrangements unintentionally signalled that 'comprehensive' was a term of convenience. To some, it also suggested that the co-existence of grammar and 'comprehensive' schools was not, after all, impossible. The operation of local interim and semi-comprehensive arrangements during the mid-1960s set a precedent – not followed in Scotland, where the central authority provided stronger leadership and pursued narrower reorganization options (see McPherson and Raab, 1988) – for the following decade. In 1969, Secretary of State Edward Short introduced a Parliamentary Bill requiring those LEAs which had not responded to Crosland's 1965 circular to do so. The Bill was lost, however, when Prime Minister Harold Wilson called a general election the following year. One of the first decisions of Short's Conservative successor, Margaret Thatcher, was to publish Circular 10/70, effectively withdrawing Labour's circular of five years earlier. The momentum of the drive for comprehensive education nevertheless continued. Indeed, Mrs Thatcher presided over more comprehensive school designations than any of her predecessors or successors in that office, although she also vetoed a total of 94 proposals from LEAs to amalgamate or close grammar schools.

Comprehensive schools were sometimes intended to replace – not compete with – grammar and secondary modern schools. This was, on the whole, the reality of the Scottish experience, but in many English and Welsh LEAs selective practices continued throughout the 1960s and 1970s. In 1970 the Conservative Chair of Birmingham LEA expressed satisfaction with Circular 10/70 on the grounds that he supported *both* comprehensive and grammar schools (*BBC television news*, 24 June 1970). Where state grammar schools continued to operate, however, comprehensives were 'comprehensive' only by aspiration. Some such institutions were, in fact, simply redesignated secondary modern schools. Even where an LEA chose to adopt a 'fully comprehensive' solution, vestiges of the former selective system could sometimes be identified. For example, according to data from 1974, comprehensive schools which had formerly been grammar schools were considerably more likely to have a sixth form than ex-secondary modern comprehensives. Clear statistical linkages were found between students in ex-grammar comprehensives having relatively high prior academic achievements, following a more traditionally academic curriculum, obtaining more public examination passes, proceeding to university and obtaining high status jobs (see Kerckhoff, Fogelman, Crook and Reeder, 1996).

CIRCULAR 4/74 AND THE 1976 EDUCATION ACT

Upon returning to office in 1974 the Labour government replaced Circular 10/70 with Circular 4/74, once again requesting LEAs to extend comprehensive schooling. A survey in February 1975 indicated that only 20 of the English and Welsh LEAs were 'truly comprehensive', and a quarter of all ten-year-old pupils still sat the 11-plus examination (Simon, 1991:439). The serious economic condition of the country had slowed the drive for comprehensive education, but by this stage Secretary of State Fred Mulley no longer shared the view of several of his predecessors that the remaining un-reorganized LEAs would fall into line. Following the decision of seven LEAs to defy the government's policy (*BBC television news*, 28 January 1975), a new Conservative administration in Tameside decided to withdraw the scheme for comprehensive education put forward by its Labour predecessors. The Secretary of State's attempted intervention to halt this reversal was subsequently ruled unlawful by the Law Lords (*BBC television news*, 2 August 1976), a decision that prompted Mulley to introduce a new Bill along the same lines as the abortive legislation from 1969-70. By the time this reached the statute book in 1976, however, Shirley Williams had succeeded Mulley in James Callaghan's government and the 'Great Debate' about the future of education was under way.

The continuing economic crisis, industrial unrest and doubts, including some at Cabinet level (Chitty, 1989:69), about the effectiveness of comprehensive education, made it very difficult to enforce the 1976 Education Act. Significantly, a 1978 DES report (DES, 1978) was more retrospective than forward-looking. It confirmed the Labour government's unwillingness to differentiate between the genuinely comprehensive and partially comprehensive solutions adopted by a number of LEAs.

COMPREHENSIVE EDUCATION, 1979-97

Following Margaret Thatcher's general election victory of May 1979, the 1976 Act was repealed by new legislation. In spite of this, the early 1980s witnessed a number of LEA secondary reorganizations along comprehensive lines, including Bolton, Tameside, Cornwall and Cumbria (Simon, 1991:482-83). Over the course of the decade the principle of comprehensive education was subjected to significant redefinition as a result of central government policies designed to promote 'choice' and 'diversity'. From 1981 the Assisted Places Scheme drew children out of the state system and into independent schools. Later, the landmark 1988 Education Act sought to promote two new types of self-governing secondary school, the City Technology College (CTC) and the Grant Maintained (GM) school. In some areas the GM school initiative proved to be a vehicle for the partial reintroduction of selection (Fitz, Halpin and Power, 1993). In a 1992 television interview the then Secretary of State, Kenneth Clarke, indicated his own support for selective schooling by stating that he had 'no objection to the re-emergence of grammar schools, if that is what parents want' (*The Times*,

3 February 1992). His successor, John Patten, suggested that another approach would be followed, however. He confirmed that the government would seek to encourage comprehensive schools to 'do a little bit of "picking and choosing" on the side, without coming to me for permission to change their character' (Patten, 1992).

An increasing number of specialist secondary schools developed in the wake of the 1992 White Paper, *Choice and Diversity* (DfE, 1992), and further legislation of the following year. These schools were permitted to select according to pupil aptitude in such areas as technology, languages or music, rather than ability. Simultaneously, Prime Minister John Major's association of comprehensive schools with 'low standards' in a letter to the former General Secretary of the National Union of Teachers (NUT) (quoted in *The Independent*, 28 February 1992; see also Jarvis, 1993). Significantly, just one specific reference to comprehensive schooling appeared in *Choice and Diversity* (DfE, 1992, 1). More surprisingly, perhaps, the 1993 report of the independent National Commission on Education (1993) also made only one reference to comprehensive education (p.25).

During the early 1990s a small number of comprehensive schools introduced grammar streams, while in 1994 the Queen Elizabeth GM School, Penrith abandoned its comprehensive status to become a fully selective grammar school. No groundswell of support for these initiatives followed, but supporters of selection received an unexpected boost in January 1996 when the Labour Party Shadow Health spokesperson, Harriet Harman, opted to send her son to a grammar school outside her immediate locality. Possibly sensing that this might be an opportune moment to inject still more choice and variety into state education under the banner of improving standards, Prime Minister John Major and his Policy Unit sketched plans for every large town in England to develop at least one GM grammar school, to be funded mostly by the private sector (*The Times*, 11 March 1996). At that year's party conference Mr Major sought further to undermine the

Labour opposition by boasting that 'We grammar school boys, Ken Clarke (the then Chancellor of the Exchequer) and I, did not have the same start in private education as Mr Blair and Miss Harman'. This strategy was to backfire when it emerged that Clarke had, in fact, been a scholarship boy at the fee-paying Nottingham High School (*Daily Telegraph*, 13 October 1996). Any sense of affection for his *alma mater*, Rutlish Grammar School, now a comprehensive, had been conspicuously absent from the foreword Mr Major contributed to an institutional history of the school one year earlier (Brock, 1995). Gillian Shephard, the Education Secretary, was also haunted by her personal past. Although she appeased some of her right-wing critics by promising to 'make it very, very much easier for there to be selective schools, grammar schools, where parents and teachers and governors want it' (*Daily Telegraph*, 10 June 1996), it was well known that, during the 1970s, Mrs Shephard had campaigned for a fully comprehensive system in Norfolk (*Daily Telegraph*, 25 June 1996). One grammar school head teacher called for her to be sacked for her alleged bias towards comprehensives after she rejected proposals to lower his school's entry age from 14 to 11, while approving a plan for a neighbouring comprehensive school to open a sixth form (*Daily Telegraph*, 13 June 1996).

A White Paper, published in June 1996, had been widely expected to make provision for a grammar school in every town. Instead, however, the document focused upon increasing the number of specialist schools, selecting on grounds of aptitude, rather than ability, and on permitting existing schools greater freedom to select. The White Paper proposed that GM schools should be able to select up to 50 per cent of their pupils, specialist schools 30 per cent and LEA comprehensives 20 per cent. These thresholds featured in a Parliamentary Bill, published in October 1996. The Bill was before Parliament at the time of the Wirral South by-election of February 1997, during which the respective political parties' policies on selective and comprehensive education received close media examination. Six grammar schools were located within the Wirral South constituency, including one attended by the former Labour Prime Minister, Harold Wilson. Plans for Secretary of State Gillian Shephard's Bill to extend selection were sacrificed in the early Spring when a general election was called. During the campaign Mrs Shephard indicated a determination to reactivate her plans at the earliest opportunity. She told BBC Radio Four's *Today* programme:

> The evidence is – and in very different areas of the country – that the existence of grammar schools pushes up standards in all schools and that, of course, is what parents want and what the country needs. (Interview on the *Today* programme, 21 April 1997, BBC Radio Four)

On 1 May, however, Mrs Shephard and her Party lost power to a Labour government, led by Prime Minister Tony Blair.

NEW LABOUR AND SELECTION

For the Labour Party comprehensive education has been a vexing issue for much of the current decade. Party soundbites from the 1992 general election suggested a renewed commitment to the abandonment of selection within the state education system and the re-assertion of LEA control over all maintained schools (see, for example, *The Independent*, 26 February 1992). Following their fourth successive general election defeat, however, the Party moved towards a position that accepted, and then embraced, diversity, not least perhaps because of Mr Blair's decision to send his sons to a GM Roman Catholic comprehensive school. In both 1995 and 1996 David Blunkett assured the Labour Party Conference that there would be no selection either by examination or interview under a Labour government, but Harriet Harman's decision to exercise her parental choice in favour of a grammar school precipitated a difficult period for Labour, resulting in the resignation of its Campaigns Director and the Chairman of the Party's Backbench

Education Committee. The then shadow Education spokesperson, David Blunkett, again confirmed that the Labour Party was against selection, but supported his colleague's personal decision (*Channel Four News*, 23 January 1996). Five months later, shortly after Tony Blair had called for much wider use of setting and 'fast-tracking' within comprehensive schools (*The Times*, 7 June 1996), Mr Blunkett indicated that a Labour government would allow parents to decide the future of grammar schools (*Channel Four News*, 25 June 1996).

During the 1997 general election campaign Mr Blair confirmed Labour's commitment to supporting parental decisions on the future of grammar schools. He told an audience in Birmingham:

> Let me say this about school structures. I have no intention of waging war on any schools except failing schools. So far as the existing 160 grammar schools are concerned, as long as the parents want them, they will stay... We will tackle what isn't working, not what is. (Speech at the Barber Institute, University of Birmingham, 14 April 1997)

Immediately after their election in May 1997 the new Labour government published proposals to allow parents to decide the fate of grammar schools. The principle of selection was, nevertheless, retained. The 1997 White Paper, *Excellence in Schools*, and the Bill, which in due course reached the statute book as the 1998 School Standards and Framework Act, endorsed the previous administration's support for specialist schools, albeit with less emphasis on their selective character. The number of specialist English secondary schools currently stands at 402. By 2003 it is anticipated that this figure will increase to 800 (*DfEE News* 496/98, 29 October 1998). The Act additionally permitted *any* school to select 10 per cent of pupils on 'aptitude' if the governing body is satisfied the school has a specialism.

The present government's policy towards comprehensive education is regarded by many as ambiguous. This may be attributed to the convergence of views from the radical right and the postmodernist left, both of which now tend 'to dismiss the comprehensive school as an institution of the past – part of the social democratic agenda of the Sixties and therefore of no relevance to the world of the Nineties' (Chitty, 1994:89). It is in this context, perhaps, that contributions to the debate about selection by apparently 'left-of-centre' writers such as Pollard (1995) and Adonis and Pollard (1997) might best be understood.

Since becoming Prime Minister, Tony Blair has conspicuously sought to distance himself and his party from the issue of grammar school ballots, laying himself open to the charge that he is trying to have it both ways. He has refused to support the closure of grammar schools that are popular with parents and espouses the development of 'modern comprehensive schools 'that' take account – for example by setting in different subjects – of different abilities without going back to the old system of the 11-plus' (interviewed on the *Jimmy Young* programme, BBC Radio Two, 9 February 1999). In a recent, heated parliamentary exchange with the opposition leader, Mr Blair objected to the comprehensive school-educated William Hague's suggestion that 'Labour Party activists' were seeking to destroy grammar schools, countering:

> the Labour government are not closing grammar schools. At present, the power to close a grammar schools lies with the local education authority. The decision then goes to the Secretary of State. Our legislation takes it out of the hands of the local education authority and puts it in the hands of the parents. The party that closed more grammar schools in Britain than any other was the Conservative party'.
> (*Hansard* H. of C., 7 July 1999, col. 1028)

It is now clear that, on this issue, the Labour government has retreated somewhat from the position outlined by David Blunkett in opposition, notwithstanding the Prime Minister's recent denial on television (interviewed on *Newsnight*, BBC television, 19 July 1999). In part, this may be related to the Blair family's personal choice to send their three children to non-local, over-subscribed schools which select Year Seven pupils by interview, though with a focus upon faith. Other difficulties in this area may yet have to be faced if ballots lead to the demise of manifestly successful schools. For example, the government's list of 'beacon' schools is potentially embarrassing. The original list of 75 schools, published on 7 July 1998, included four schools – three secondary moderns and one grammar – which, as a result of a ballot, may experience redesignation before their three-year status as beacon schools expires. Currently a total of five grammar schools, around 3 per cent of the total – had been awarded beacon school status (*Hansard* H. of C. written answer by Estelle Morris, 20 May 1999). In a separate exercise of 'naming and acclaiming', 14 grammar schools were among 66 to be praised by Ofsted in a report of February 1999 (*Daily Telegraph*, 12 February 1999).

3
Selective versus comprehensive education: a review of research and other writings

INTRODUCTION: THE NATURE OF RESEARCH AND OTHER COMMENTARIES

During the late 1950s and early 1960s the conclusions drawn by a number of influential research studies were used to challenge the principle of selective secondary schooling. As Harold Silver (1994:77) notes, Floud, Halsey and Martin's (1956) work on the relationship between social class 'was followed by a considerable literature which analysed the nature of existing secondary school provision, the factors militating against working-class children gaining access to and succeeding in grammar school education, and pointed to the solution that was gaining political and educational ground – the comprehensive secondary school'. Selection, it was argued, was a major cause of 'social waste' in that it advantaged the children of middle-class parents and was an impediment to equality (Jackson and Marsden, 1962; Douglas, 1964; Dale and Griffith, 1965). Selection tests were also reported to be unreliable indicators of children's potential. In 1957 a committee of leading psychologists, headed by P.E. Vernon and including Hans Eysenck (who was later to adopt a very different position), challenged the disciples of psychometric testing by arguing that human intelligence could be influenced by environment and by upbringing. The report concluded that: 'Any policy involving irreversible segregation at eleven years or earlier is psychologically unsound, and therefore...in so far as public opinion allows – the common or comprehensive school would be preferable, at least up to the age of thirteen' (Vernon, 1957:43-44, 53, quoted in Simon, 1991:209). In the same year a major NFER report noted that in some LEAs as many as 45 per cent of 11-year-olds proceeded to a grammar school, while the figure was as low as 10 per cent elsewhere. Even the most carefully devised selection procedures, it was maintained, had an error margin of 10 per cent. This pointed to the conclusion that around 60,000 children per annum were allocated to the 'wrong' secondary school (Yates and Pidgeon, 1957:191-93).

Over the past 30 years research into selective and comprehensive secondary school systems may broadly be classified into six categories:

- sociological studies of selective and comprehensive education (e.g.Ford, 1969; Ball (ed), 1984)

- historical studies of the development of comprehensive education (e.g. Rubinstein and Simon, 1969; Fenwick, 1976)

- surveys detailing current national secondary education trends (e.g. Benn, annually 1967-72; Monks, 1968)

- ethnographic studies of particular schools (e.g. Hargreaves, 1967; Lacey, 1970; Ball, 1981; Burgess, 1983; Palmer, 1998)

- case studies of individual LEA secondary education policies (see, for example, those listed in Fearn, 1980, 1983 and 1989; James, 1980)

- studies comparing the performance of selective and comprehensive schools and school systems.

The remainder of this section of the review focuses upon studies in the final category listed above. The earliest efforts to compare selective and comprehensive school systems, such as those attempted by Koshe (1957), Pedley (1969) and Baldwin (1975), as well as a number of local studies, were crude and methodologically flawed (Reynolds and Sullivan with Murgatroyd, 1987:35-38). From the 1970s, however, such studies generally began to draw upon a wider range of data and employed more advanced analytical and statistical techniques. But even with the increasing availability and accessibility of performance data and indicators of the 'value-added' contribution of secondary schools, the problems of measuring institutional and system-level performance have not disappeared. Contemporary criticisms concerning the adequacy or otherwise of the government's approach to measuring school improvement and effectiveness mirror the arguments relating to the significance of socio-economic variables adopted in the research studies discussed below.

Before examining in detail the most significant studies seeking to compare comprehensive and selective schooling some cautionary words are necessary. It should be understood that this area of educational research has been fraught with difficulties. Since the publication of the first two anti-comprehensive Black Papers on education (Cox and Dyson, 1969a, 1969b) debates about the nature and organization of secondary education in England have been highly politicized. A number of the researchers who have contributed studies have been accused of allowing their own ideological or political positions to colour their findings. In instances where relevant affiliations of the individuals in question are known, these are noted in the text below, as are the strengths and weaknesses of the chosen methodologies. It is, however, impossible to be absolutely certain about whether, and to what extent, researchers' personal starting points have influenced their published findings.

Benn and Simon (1970; second edition 1972)

Half Way There, the title of this 1970 research study, appropriately reflected the authors' personal positions on the question of comprehensive education. The book reported findings from a major 1968 survey of comprehensive schools in England, Scotland and Wales. Many of the data included in the book were gathered from responses to a very substantial school questionnaire. The authors also conducted interviews with head teachers, staff, parents, pupils and administrators. The book is divided into three parts. The first part sets out the national and international background to the drive for comprehensive education. The second examines the various types of comprehensive schemes and schools to emerge from the process of secondary reorganization. Three basic models of 'going comprehensive' were identified, based upon:

- schemes for 11-18 'all-through' schools

- tiered schemes involving a system of first (5-8 or 5-9), middle (8-12 or 9-13) and high schools (post-12 or post-13)

- schemes incorporating separate sixth-form (post-16) colleges.

The third part of the book analyses the internal organization of comprehensive schools. Overall, the book conveys a snapshot of British education in the midst of upheaval and change. A range of tables confirmed considerable variation in relation to such areas as the age ranges, size, curriculum, pastoral system and management structure of comprehensive schools. The authors did not regard the diversity of these comprehensive 'solutions' as a particular weakness. What mattered, they suggested, was that the principle of comprehensive education had been 'accepted by the great majority of the teaching profession, parents, and students themselves, and by all political parties' (Benn and Simon, 1972 edition:490).

It might reasonably be assumed that the authors of *Half Way There*, both of whom were – and continue to be – prominent campaigners for comprehensive and state education, were seeking to accelerate the trend towards non-selection. The study indicated that reorganized or reorganizing LEAs had deployed a wide variety of approaches and solutions. In order to advance from a position of 'half way there' to a fully comprehensive system the authors wished to encourage those LEAs that had thus far retained selection to understand the benefits of comprehensive education.

The nature of the data included in *Half Way There* did not lend itself to a direct comparison between secondary selective and comprehensive systems. Notwithstanding this, and also the fact that the data reported in the study are now more than 30 years old, the authors' conclusions about the coexistence of selective and comprehensive schools in partially reorganized areas may be of some relevance to the current situation in LEAs where there are still secondary grammar, modern and comprehensive schools. The authors concluded that 'where systematic coexistence remains there are no genuine comprehensive schools' (Benn and Simon, 1972 edition:491).

Steedman (1980)

This research, by a staff member at the National Children's Bureau (NCB), was commissioned by the DES to 'evaluate aspects of educational progress in selective and non selective secondary schools' in England (Steedman, 1980:1). It drew upon data from the National Child Development Study (NCDS) of individuals born between 3 and 9 March 1958. The NCDS developed from a 'Perinatal Mortality Survey' of data relating to 17,733 babies. Follow-up data collections were made at the ages of seven, 11, 16, 20, 23 and 33 by means of questionnaires focusing upon education, employment, family and health matters. Steedman's study, entitled *Progress in Secondary Schools*, drew upon the data sweep for 1974, when members of the NCDS cohort were 16 years old. At that time, over half the cohort members attended secondary comprehensive schools. The NCDS offered unique information, therefore, about large numbers of the children and their schools. Recognizing, however, that it may be unfair to compare the performance of children in recently established comprehensive schools with those attending long-established selective schools, the author limited the sample to include only those children who had spent their entire secondary school careers in a school whose status did not change.

Like other longitudinal data sets, the NCDS contained key information about the characteristics of children before they entered secondary school. These data revealed that NCDS pupils who entered comprehensive schools at the age of 11 were relatively disadvantaged in terms of skill levels in reading and mathematics, and also in terms of their social class backgrounds. Multivariate analyses were conducted to adjust for these initial disadvantages, as a result of which Steedman concluded that differences in the rate of pupil progress in selective and comprehensive school systems were not statistically significant.

Press coverage of Steedman's report focused on the discovery that the progress made by the most able children in comprehensive schools in reading and mathematics matched that of their counterparts in the grammar schools (see Steedman, 1987:178). The pro-comprehensive lobby used this finding to challenge allegations made in the Black Papers that able children were disadvantaged by a comprehensive school education. Others were unconvinced, however. In a withering attack on the research, published by the right-wing think tank, the Centre for Policy Studies, Caroline Cox and John Marks (1980) suggested that the author was biased in favour of comprehensive schools and accused the NCB of 'news management'. In fact, the report had not unconditionally supported the performance of comprehensive schools. Concern had been expressed, for example, that children of average ability did not perform as well as might be hoped in comprehensive schools. The criticisms of Cox and Marks attracted a vigorous rebuttal from the NCB (Steedman, Fogelman and Hutchison, 1980) on the grounds that the study's findings had been both misunderstood and misrepresented.

It might be noted that this study, whatever its possible imperfections, sought to take account of pupils' academic capabilities prior to entering their secondary school. The success of English secondary schools has long been measured in terms of public examination performance, without taking account – other than pass/fail 11-plus test records and (sometimes) primary school reports – of pupils' abilities upon entry. The availability of National Curriculum test results for Key Stages One and Two and improved feeder school liaison offer the prospect of more satisfactory judgements of pupils' progress in secondary schools.

Marks, Cox and Pomian-Szrednicki (1983)

This study was published by the independently funded National Council for Educational Standards (NCES), an offshoot of the National Council for Academic Standards, founded in 1972 by a number of high-profile journalists, academics and Black Paper authors (Griggs, 1989:107-8). The authors made use of the 1981 public examination results for English selective and comprehensive schools, the first such data to be published under the terms of the 1980 Education Act. Two major measures or 'benchmarks' of examination performance were used: the number of O level and CSE grade 1 passes per pupil and the average number of examination points per pupil according to an attainment scale applied to both examinations. The first measure focused upon higher ability children while the second was used in relation to the full ability range.

In their analyses the authors sought to control for a range of variables, including social class, LEA expenditure and pupils from non-English-speaking backgrounds, by using multiple regression analyses. The 54 English LEAs included in the study were also grouped into three 'relatively homogeneous' categories in order to facilitate comparisons between areas with similar percentages from social class groupings (Marks, Cox and Pomian-Szrednicki, 1983:39). According to both measures used in the study the performance of comprehensive school pupils was below the national average. Unsurprisingly, grammar school pupils performed best. Comprehensive school pupils performed better than those attending secondary modern schools, but it was noted that pupils in the latter type of school did better than expected (pp.49-51). It was reported that the number of examination passes per pupil in a selective system of grammar and secondary modern schools was between 30 per cent and 40 per cent higher than that achieved by pupils in a fully comprehensive system (pp.55-61). The average results of pupils in comprehensive schools within the same LEA were also found to vary considerably (p.19).

The methodology used by Marks, Cox and Pomian-Szrednicki has been heavily criticized. Even the authors themselves have acknowledged that the original aim of the research differed from that of the published study. A census of the results of all secondary schools in England and Wales had been the original intention, but the authors were unable to secure the help of sufficient LEAs for this to be feasible (Marks and Cox, 1984:11). Clifford and Heath (1984) have argued that the authors' method of controlling for social class did not adequately reflect differences in social class intakes of schools within LEAs (Clifford and Heath, 1984:91). According to Gray and Jesson (1989:91), a major weakness of this study is that 'By confining itself to measures of social disadvantage it ignored measures of social advantage, which have been found to be more important in explaining the higher levels of performance'. In 1984 Gray, Jesson and Jones re-examined some of the same data, and reached substantially different conclusions (see sections 4.25-4.26 below). Perhaps the most questionable aspect of this study is the attempt made by Marks, Cox and Pomian-Szrednicki – on the basis of limited evidence – to predict what fully selective and fully comprehensive national systems might look like. According to Clifford and Heath (1984:93) the introduction of alternative, equally justifiable, controlling variables would point to substantially different conclusions being drawn from the same data set. In terms of its methodology this study has been described as the weakest of the several NCES investigations into selective and comprehensive education (Gray and Jesson, 1989:91).

Those currently wishing to preserve grammar schools from the possibility of closure and amalgamation are likely to be attracted to the findings from this study. Without advocating an end to comprehensive schools it seriously questioned their success and called instead for a diverse mix of selective and non-selective schools.

Steedman (1983)

This NCB study, an extension of the DES research reported three years earlier, compared the public examination results of pupils aged 16 attending established comprehensive, secondary modern and grammar schools. Steedman found that 'raw' or uncorrected results placed grammar schools well ahead of other secondary schools, with 5.12 O level equivalent passes per pupil. Comprehensives came next with an average of 1.60, and secondary moderns came last, obtaining 0.98 O level equivalents per pupil (Steedman, 1983:78). However, after making allowances for differences in attainment at age 11, pupils' social class and parental interest, these differences were much reduced. The ranking of the three types of school remained the same, but the difference between the grammar and comprehensive schools was reduced to 0.92, and that between the comprehensive and secondary modern schools was reduced to 0.28.

In another analysis Steedman aggregated the results of the grammar and secondary modern schools and compared the overall average for this combination of schools with that of the comprehensives alone. Before correcting for differences in family background and initial attainment at age 11, the grammar/modern combination obtained better overall results. After controlling for these factors no differences were found to be statistically significant. In conclusion, Steedman noted that 'There was no sign from these results that selection, in the sense of having a mixture of grammars and secondary moderns, could be said to have made a difference to examination performance' (Steedman, 1983:133).

In their critiques of this study Marks and Cox (1984:16) and Marks and Pomian-Szrednicki (1985:96) noted that Steedman's sample of 2,896 children was even smaller than the number featuring in her 1980 study. Marks and Pomian-Szrednicki especially doubted whether the 127 comprehensive school pupils from the top 20 per cent ability range constituted a sufficiently large or representative sample. In both studies Steedman restricted her analyses to pupils attending schools which had not changed status during their period of attendance, but the second NCB investigation was further restricted by difficulties in tracing the examination results for some pupils. Clifford and Heath (1984) also expressed reservations about the exclusivity of Steedman's sample. Notwithstanding their criticisms of some aspects of the 1983 NCES study they argued that Steedman might usefully have enlarged the NCDS sample by following the example of Marks, Cox and Pomian-Szrednicki (1983) in grouping pupils by LEA type. In relation to Steedman's approach, they comment that:

Some of the reductions are quite proper – the restriction to England, for example, or the exclusion of children who attended independent schools. However, there is the worry that there has been some distortion in the sample over and above these deliberate exclusions. (p.90)

It might be noted that Steedman's stated purpose was not directly to compare selective and comprehensive systems. Indeed, she was cautious in explaining that:

This study was of a particular period (1969 to 1974) in the piecemeal changeover to comprehensive schooling, at which time there was no fully comprehensive system…It must…be emphasized at the start that the findings of this study concerning schools called comprehensive may not generalize to present day comprehensive schools. They are observations of how pupils were faring in schools which were not true comprehensives but which coexisted with selective schools (Steedman, 1983:3).

Gray, McPherson and Raffe (1983)

This book, written by Edinburgh University researchers, studied secondary education in Scotland since 1945. Comparisons were made between public examination results of selective and comprehensive schools, but this section comprises a relatively small part of the book. The sample of Scottish Certificate of Education Highers and O-grade examination results was based on a postal survey of 40 per cent of the 1975-76 school leavers in four of the nine regions of Scotland. The total number of respondents was 16,926, approximately 20 per cent of all the school leavers in Scotland for that year. Controls were included for pupils' social class, but no information about the prior achievements or ability of the pupils was available to the authors.

The study divided schools into two groups: the 'uncreamed comprehensive sector' and the 'selective sector'. In their conclusions, the authors noted that:

> the data would suggest that comprehensive education had a levelling effect on attainment, raising fewer pupils to the highest levels of attainment, but helping more of them to progress beyond the minimum. It appears to have raised average attainment, although the definition of this average clearly depends on the relative importance of different levels of attainment implied by our scale. (Gray, McPherson and Raffe, 1983:256)

The authors found not only higher average attainment but also a lower level of social class inequality in the uncreamed comprehensive sector (p.257). They argued, however, that the success of comprehensive education did not derive from the post-1965 reorganization but from the democratic, community tradition of Scottish schooling (p.266), an issue that has subsequently been discussed at greater length by Lindsay Paterson (1997).

The authors' decision to classify comprehensive schools located close to maintained, grant-aided or independent selective institutions as 'creamed' schools is the most controversial methodological feature of this study. Nearly 50 per cent of the pupils in the sample attending comprehensive schools were attending such 'creamed' comprehensives in 1975-76. These individuals are therefore included in the 'selective' sector, comprising some 11,615 pupils. The remaining 5,236 comprehensive pupils included in the study attended schools in primarily rural areas. These schools and pupils formed the 'uncreamed comprehensive sector'. The authors were careful to justify this methodological starting point, but its validity was questioned by Marks and Cox (1984:19), who found it incredible that the authors classified comprehensive schools located in such areas as Dundee, Edinburgh and Glasgow within the 'selective sector'.

Gray, Jesson and Jones (1984)

In a 1984 special issue of the *Oxford Review of Education,* a team of researchers from Sheffield University conducted a parallel analysis of the data studied in the first NCES publication by Marks, Cox and Pomian-Szrednicki (1983). The latter study, it was maintained, had inadequately made allowance for pupils' social class and other related factors, including school organization. Deploying a range of statistical controls adjudged to be more satisfactory than those used in the NCES study, the authors concluded that there was no reason to suppose that selective secondary systems would produce superior pupil examination results (Gray, Jesson and Jones, 1984:56). Calculations by the authors also led them to doubt whether Marks, Cox and Pomian-Szrednicki had made sufficient allowance for 'comprehensive' schools which did not admit the full ability range of pupils (pp.57-59).

In a short discussion at the end of the article the authors regret the imperfections of the data used by a succession of researchers. These and other difficulties are briefly discussed in the commentary at the end of Part Four.

Department of Education and Science (1983 and 1984)

In 1983 the DES published *Statistical Bulletin* 16/83, entitled 'School standards and spending: statistical analysis', which considered the associations between measures of socio-economic background of pupils in maintained LEA schools, LEA secondary school expenditure and the average levels of pupil attainment in public examinations at age 16. A range of statistics was published for each English and Welsh LEA, together with some summary findings. It was concluded that variations in pupils' public examination attainment could not strongly be correlated with the secondary school expenditure of the LEA.

This study was criticized (for example by Marks and Pomian-Szrednicki, 1985:104) for making no attempt to include selectivity as a factor that may have a bearing upon pupils' public examination results at age 16. This omission was redressed one year later when *Statistical Bulletin* 13/84 sought further to refine and review the statistical investigation. A total of six measures of pupil examination success were used, drawing upon data from the DES's School Leavers' Survey. This investigation deployed a wider range of controls for socio-economic background factors and expenditure variables than the earlier study. The analysis was once again aggregated to the LEA level on the grounds that appropriate data were not available below this level of aggregation.

Statistical Bulletin 13/84 reported a stronger than anticipated positive association between grammar school attendance and pupil examination attainment at age 16. Supporters of grammar schools are likely to conclude from this research that the interests of high ability pupils are best served in a grammar school environment. But, while the DES statisticians included a grammar school measure, they did not include ones for comprehensive or secondary modern schools. Conclusions about statistical associations, therefore, can only be made at the 'top end' and it cannot be deduced from this short report what sort of arrangements might be best for other pupils. The *Bulletin* is significant, however, in one important respect: it confirmed that the DES had become more interested in analysing the relative performance of pupils in selective and comprehensive schools. During the early part of the 1980s, according to a savage critique by Caroline Cox and John Marks (1988), civil servants had been contemptuous of any attempt to question the success of comprehensive education. Overall, though, this report, produced largely for the use of DES financial officers, throws very little light upon the issues under consideration here.

Marks and Pomian-Szrednicki (1985)

Standards in English Schools, the second report by the NCES, was published in 1985. The research design closely followed that of the 1983 study. The public examination results of some 380,000 pupils in more than 2,000 schools and 57 LEAs were analysed, making this 'the largest school-based study yet undertaken in this country' (Marks and Pomian-Szrednicki, 1985:8). The results mirrored the findings of the earlier study: pupils in the best-performing LEAs achieved three times the average number of O level passes of their counterparts in the worst-performing LEAs. Comparisons between LEAs with similar social class compositions also revealed significant variations.

Selectivity was found to be a statistically significant variable, even after allowance had been made for social class. The authors' finding that 'pupils in selective schools still seem generally to attain more and better passes than those in comprehensives' (p.14) suggested to them that questions might usefully be asked about the success of comprehensive education. The same national 'benchmarks' referred to in the 1983 study were again used. Once again, those LEAs which contained a relatively high percentage of grammar school pupils performed best according to the measure of average number of O level and CSE grade 1 passes per pupil. The second measure of points per pupil, acknowledged by the authors as being a useful indicator of attainment levels for all pupils (p.19), revealed no significant differences between comprehensive and selective organizations, however. As Gray and Jesson have observed (1989:92), it is a curiosity that Marks and Pomian-Szrednicki do not discuss this latter finding.

Marks, Cox and Pomian-Szrednicki (1986)

This third NCES study of examination performance of ILEA secondary schools, using the authors' now familiar passes and points-per-pupil approach, began by noting that several recent reports relating to education in the capital had shown that 'all has not been well' (Marks, Cox and Pomian-Szrednicki, 1986:7). Consistent with the 1983 and 1985 national NCES studies it was acknowledged that it would be 'a nonsense' to compare schools of different types or with different social class intakes (p.8). Information published annually by ILEA until 1980 concerning the educational abilities of pupils entering their secondary schools was used as a control (pp.51-52). The authors suggested that this made it possible for them to identify genuinely 'comprehensive' schools with a full ability, as well as comprehensive schools that were 'more akin to the former secondary modern schools' (p.8). The authors demonstrated some familiarity with the unique and diverse socio-economic composition of London, observing that areas of great deprivation, such as Stepney and Tower Hamlets, stood in stark contrast to the affluent suburbs of Hampstead, Highgate and Dulwich. The latter areas, it was noted, were populated by 'families of the intelligentsia and the prestigious professionals, by no means all of whom send their children to independent schools' (p.8).

These perceived advantages, and also the relatively generous level of resources allocated to ILEA schools (p.53), were not reflected in the public examination results achieved by ILEA pupils. Even on the basis of comparison with socially-deprived LEAs, ILEA's performance was found to be poor. Pupils attending ILEA's comprehensive schools, the authors concluded, were performing worse than their counterparts attending both comprehensive and secondary modern schools elsewhere in England (pp.22-23).

The authors themselves acknowledged some limitations relating to this research. For example, they were unable 'to relate examination results to other social and educational variables like expenditure, social class, test scores, ethnic origins of pupils and various school factors' (p.62). Neither did they acknowledge or seek to engage with the criticisms made by Gray, Jesson and Jones (1984) concerning the viability of grouping LEAs according to their assumed social class homogeneity. More surprisingly, no account was taken of London's very strong independent school sector.

The study contained no direct comparison of selective and non-selective schools on the grounds that 'All the secondary schools in ILEA are comprehensive schools' (p.22). Not everyone would agree with this starting point, however. For example, in 1996, Sir Peter Newsam, a former Education Officer for London, argued that 'secondary education in inner London is not, as a system, "comprehensive" and never has been; it is both diverse and highly selective'. Of the 49 'genuine' inner London comprehensive schools, Newsam argued, the majority were performing above average national performance levels in terms of pupils attaining five or more A-C grades at GCSE (Newsam, 1996).

The purpose of this research by Marks, Cox and Pomian-Szrednicki is unclear. Some readers may be drawn to the unstated conclusion that comprehensive schooling and low standards are associated. By implication, the report encourages readers to consider the possible advantages (and disadvantages) of differentiated secondary schooling.

McPherson and Willms (1987)

Like the earlier Edinburgh University study (Gray, McPherson and Raffe, 1983), this article, published in the journal *Sociology*, provided strong support for comprehensive education in Scotland. A positive picture was presented of working-class pupils – and girls, in particular – benefiting from 'equalization and improvement' as a result of comprehensive school attendance, although the authors acknowledged the possibility that other factors may have contributed to this change.

The data sources and analysis used in the research design were generally of a higher quality than the earlier Scottish study. The authors examined national representative samples of Scottish school-leavers from 1976, 1980 and 1984 and were drawn to the conclusion that, once comprehensive schools had become established in Scotland, they contributed to a rise in educational attainment and diminished the influence of social class factors.

Arguably, rather too much significance has been attached to this piece of research. Interestingly, two Scottish head teachers have recently disclaimed credit for their schools' performance table success on the grounds that this derives, to a considerable degree, from such factors as social composition and catchment area (see Duffield, 1998). The usefulness of relating research findings from Scotland and elsewhere to the English context is further considered later.

Reynolds, Sullivan with Murgatroyd (1987)

This was a relatively small-scale study of 'Treliw', a south Wales community which experienced a partial reorganization of its nine secondary schools in the mid-1970s. Thereafter, one-third of pupils remained in a selective system of grammar and secondary modern schools, while the majority attended comprehensive schools. The co-existence of two school systems within a relatively homogeneous area, recruiting very similar groups of pupils, together with the fact that the researchers had access to data relating to school intakes, made this a unique piece of research.

In 1978 15-year-olds attending all secondary schools of Treliw were tested on their verbal ability. The test scores were analysed by the authors of the study, who reported significantly higher average scores in the grammar and secondary modern schools. The relatively poor performance of the comprehensive schools was attributed to such factors as their large size, the lack of pupil involvement in school matters, inadequate pastoral care provision, inadequate contact with parents, over-strict discipline and an over-emphasis upon academic, rather than social, development. It was concluded that comprehensive education is least effective when it slavishly seeks to imitate the grammar school tradition. The authors therefore called for a new conception of comprehensive education and set out an agenda for more effective comprehensive schooling (pp.106-32).

This study may also be seen in the context of a movement that has variously sought to 'rescue', 're-define' and 'affirm' the principle of comprehensive education (see, for example, the titles of books by Barker, 1986; Chitty, 1987 and Pring and Walford, 1997).

Marks (1991)

In this wide-ranging critique of English education, published by the Social Market Foundation, Marks regretted the absence of any specially commissioned government study of relative pupil performance in comprehensive and selective schools.

The pamphlet reported no new research, but drew attention to the relatively superior performance of secondary school pupils in Northern Ireland, Germany and Japan. In the former two instances he speculated that the endurance of selective secondary education may be responsible for higher educational standards. Northern Ireland's many denominational schools and Germany's technical schools were also identified as positive features of those education systems (pp.11-12). The relevance of comparative studies is briefly discussed below.

This pamphlet was more overtly sceptical of comprehensive education than the earlier studies with which the author was associated, yet it was notably cautious in drawing specific conclusions about research evidence. Curiously, Marks's short literature survey (p.10) made reference to some of the earlier findings of Steedman (1980 and 1983), without mentioning in detail his own research findings for the NCES. He reaches 'the unfortunate but increasingly probable conclusion that the comprehensive revolution may have handicapped the education of the very pupils it was meant to help'. He also advised that:

> the elevation of social class into the central position in the debate is mistaken. The crucial questions to ask about pupils and their education are surely not about what social class they come from, but

rather about whether their abilities and aptitudes are being recognized and encouraged. (p.12)

Marks noted that, during the late 1980s and early 1990s, a number of key figures from the political left had moved closer to his own position, having concluded that comprehensive education had failed to improve opportunities for less academic and socially-disadvantaged pupils. The key to raising educational standards, he suggested, rested upon learning from school effectiveness studies and in shifting towards market-led education policies. These have indeed been key dimensions of education policy from the late 1980s, as interest in raising educational standards has eclipsed ideological attachments to structures.

Benn and Chitty (1996)

This book, written by two pro-comprehensive education activists, was a follow-up to *Half Way There* (Benn and Simon, 1970). As in the earlier work, data were mostly gathered as a result of schools (and further education colleges) completing an extensive questionnaire in 1994. The 1994 questionnaire was much longer than the 1968 version, running to 148 questions, some with additional sub-questions to provide further information. Some of the questions took the same form as the 1968 survey, but most were new (p.xi). The authors expressed satisfaction that 35 per cent of the 5,000-plus schools and colleges completed the questionnaire (p.xii). Compared with a success rate of 81 per cent in 1968, however, it might be suggested that the authors were over-optimistic in expecting head teachers and principals to participate in an elaborate and time-consuming survey.

The objectives of this very lengthy volume, running to more than 500 pages, are manifold. It traces the history of comprehensive education at the local, national and international levels and calls for a renewed commitment to the comprehensive ideal, 30 years on from Anthony Crosland's Circular 10/65. The richness of the data derived from the questionnaire is extraordinary and unique: statistics abound in relation to almost every imaginable aspect of school size, organization, ethos and management.

There is no attempt directly to compare the effectiveness of comprehensive and selective secondary school systems, although the efforts of others to do so, including a number of the research studies examined in this report, are reviewed in the early part of the book. It is, however, of interest to note the authors' findings that, whereas in the 1960s over 50 per cent of comprehensive schools were 'creamed' by one or more grammar school, the proportion had fallen to 14 per cent in 1994. Clearly, this reflected the national trend since that time to reorganize the pattern of secondary education along comprehensive lines.

Selection was, nevertheless, reported to be a strong feature of English education in the 1990s. As a result of such recent initiatives as GM and specialist schools, CTCs and open enrolment the authors conclude that 'it is unofficial – or "hidden" – selection' that constitutes today's 'great problem' (p.464).

Kerckhoff, Fogelman, Crook and Reeder (1996)

There were two purposes of this historical investigation. First, ten case studies of contrasting LEAs were investigated in order to illustrate and explain why Circular 10/65 met with such varied local responses. Explanations were offered as to why certain types of LEA preferred one kind of reorganization model rather than another. The second purpose, more relevant to this report, was to examine the impact of change from a predominantly selective to a predominantly comprehensive secondary school system upon schools and students in England and Wales. Data on schools and students came from the National Child Development Study, some of which had been used by Steedman (1980 and 1983).

The study recognized difficulties in defining a comprehensive school;

data from the 1974 NCDS sweep indicated that the youngest students in comprehensive schools ranged in age from 11 to 14, and the oldest from 16 to 18. Very few LEAs were found to have adopted a uniform reorganization model across the administrative area and considerable variations in the proportion of NCDS students preparing for public examinations at age 16 or 18 in comprehensive schools were identified, both between and within LEAs. It was noted that, in 1974, most comprehensive schools in England and Wales were operating in a system affected to some degree by selection.

The research provided clear evidence of continuity from the selective system to the comprehensive system. Students attending comprehensives without sixth forms more often came from manual family backgrounds, and they had significantly lower age 11 scores on ability and achievement tests. Their academic achievements by the end of secondary school were also significantly lower than those in the same LEAs who had attended comprehensives with sixth forms.

Further analyses revealed no significant differences in the average achievements of students at selective and comprehensive schools after controlling for socio-economic backgrounds and prior academic achievements. There was, however, clear evidence of difference in the achievements of students of different ability. High ability students performed at higher levels in the selective system and low ability students performed at higher levels in comprehensive schools. For most students, however, the degree of difference would be very small.

The book concludes with some thoughts about the contemporary difficulties facing comprehensive education. It is suggested that an overall increase in resources for comprehensive education could both raise average achievement levels and bring the achievement levels of high ability comprehensive school pupils closer to those found in the best performing selective schools. Although the Treasury has released additional funds to schools and LEAs during the past 18 months these new resources are mostly tied to specific national projects, including the literacy and numeracy drives. There may be a prospect of additional funds aimed at raising comprehensive school standards in the new Education Action Zones, but the prospect of financial inducements for selective LEAs and GM schools to 'go comprehensive' seems remote.

Marks (1998)

This study by John Marks, his second publication for the Social Market Foundation, set out to examine 1997 National Curriculum test results and GCSE grades for children aged seven to 16 in 23,000 English schools. The study also included case studies and 'report cards' for four LEAs: Barnsley, Birmingham, Buckinghamshire and Milton Keynes.

According to Marks the 1997 data revealed that standards in English schools 'are perilously low and, even worse, extremely variable'. The text of this 'Memorandum' consists mostly of a call for urgent remedial action to raise literacy and numeracy levels. Among the solutions Marks offers are more setting and streaming, the withdrawal of special educational needs pupils from mainstream classes and more didactic teaching.

The report commented remarkably little upon comprehensive schools, but concluded by stating that a link between educational standards and structures cannot be denied (p.13) and that 'it is now time to abandon policies based on aspirations for a system of schools all of the same type' (p.14). It is unlikely that this very general study can contribute greatly to the debate about the positive contribution of grammar schools, but those who argue that the promises of comprehensive education have not been realized may be attracted to it.

UK AND EUROPEAN EXPERIENCE

The absence of sufficiently 'pure' selective and comprehensive areas of England has led some commentators to examine the wider national and international dimensions of the issue. For example, there continues to be interest in comparing the predominantly comprehensive English system with the wholly selective Northern Irish experience. Marks (reported in Lee, 1999:7) has implied that the fact that 10% more children in Northern Ireland than England gain 5 A*-C GCSEs is evidence of the shortcomings of a comprehensive system. Immediately, however, potential researchers will encounter an obstacle. The meaningfulness of such a raw comparison is questionable when the demography and social composition of Northern Ireland is so different from that of England. The strong tradition of sectarian schooling in Northern Ireland – less than 2 per cent of primary and secondary children in the province currently attend integrated schools (Moser, 1997:18) – presents difficulties in pursuing a like for like comparison.

It should be noted that levels of support for the selective system in Northern Ireland are affected by the part of the system people are in. A 1992 *Channel Four News* report (5 May, 1992) focused upon two families respectively sending their children to grammar and secondary modern schools in Belfast. Unsurprisingly, the head teacher of the former school attributed her pupils' excellent public examination results to the Northern Irish system, in which as many as 40 per cent of children gain a grammar school place. The principal of a local high school, meanwhile, argued that too many of his pupils left school without qualifications, a view endorsed by the Director of the Northern Ireland Economic Research Centre, who favoured a fully comprehensive system. The overall level of support for the present system in Northern Ireland is unclear, partly because surveys have not asked directly comparable questions. According to one reported by Hillman (1994:391) a majority of parents favour the introduction of a fully comprehensive system. However, it was also reported, in 1995, that a majority of parents in the province wished to retain grammar schools (*Education*, 31 March 1995:8).

Those who favour a national system of comprehensive education (see, for example, Benn and Chitty, 1996:471) are more naturally drawn to the example of Scotland, where a fully comprehensive secondary school system boasts high academic standards. We have included two studies from Scotland (Gray, McPherson and Raffe, 1983 and McPherson and Willms, 1987) because they are so widely cited. Once again, however, different traditions and cultures militate against straightforward comparison with the English situation.

Elsewhere in Europe, there is no clear trend. The Republic of Ireland and most of the Scandinavian countries operate comprehensive school systems, while Austria, Belgium, Germany, the Netherlands and Switzerland all have selective secondary systems of one sort or another – although the age at which selection occurs is often later than 11 years.

COMMENTARY

Which type of school system – selective or comprehensive – is more effective? While this appears to be a straightforward question, a succession of research studies over a period of more than 30 years has failed to produce a consensus. In part this is because passions run so high on this issue. There is a tendency for those who support comprehensive schools to find that a comprehensive system can cater for *all* students without 'holding back' the most able. In contrast, those who wish to defend a selective system are more likely to find that students in grammar *and* secondary modern schools do better than those in comprehensive schools. Some of the methodological difficulties are fundamental, such as the inability to define a comprehensive school. Others are more complex, such as the problems associated with classifying comprehensive schools as 'uncreamed' or 'creamed'. During the past 30 years the absence of the necessary preconditions for a serious and successful study of this question have rendered it unanswerable. This is likely to remain the case now that the number of selective schools has declined to a level 'where further meaningful comparisons between systems are impossible' (Walford, 1994:23).

Caution, therefore, must be exercised in relating conclusions from earlier studies to the current situation in LEA areas where grammar schools continue to operate. Many of the data are now old and may tell us more about the changing educational landscape of past decades than the strengths and weaknesses of current arrangements. Moreover, the complexity of factors is such that clear-cut judgements and predictions about individual schools' performance cannot be made.

Nevertheless, it is possible to distil some general conclusions from the research studies which appear to be least partisan. Some of the studies also use data that are likely to be more reliable than others. As Gray, Jesson and Jones (1984) argue, it is essential either to make sure that the intakes of different systems are comparable or to make sure that there are enough data on the intakes so that statistical adjustments can be made to assess relative performance. The research by Marks, Cox and Pomian-Srzednicki, for example, does not fulfil these criteria. Kerckhoff, Fogelman, Crook and Reeder (1996) put forward three studies which do – Reynolds and Sullivan with Murgatroyd (1987), Gray, McPherson and Raffe (1983) and Steedman (1980 and 1983). Although these are not consistent in their findings, they are likely to be more robust than some of the other studies cited in this report.

These more reliable studies, and the further analysis of the NCDS data undertaken by Kerckhoff, Fogelman, Crook and Reeder (1996), indicate that the difference between the two systems is small. Indeed, the latter analysis demonstrates that *the average output, or 'system productivity', of selective and comprehensive systems is much the same.* However, there would appear to be variations at school level which suggest that *more able children do better in grammar schools and less able children do better in comprehensive schools.*[1] It needs to be noted, though, that *even in these cases the differences are very small.* It also needs to be noted that *studies found larger differences between the results of different schools of the same type than between the average results of different systems.* However, even if one accepts a system-level tendency, it cannot then be assumed that the 'superior' achievements of the academically able arise from the selective nature of the grammar schools rather than, for instance, the more favourable resourcing and teacher retention rates associated with these schools. The evidence certainly suggests that promoting higher achievement across the board will require more than a change of school admissions policies alone.

NOTE

1. As this book was going to press, new research by Jesson was reported to show that 'brighter pupils "do better" at comprehensives' (*The Times*, 2 November 1999). Analysis of able pupils' performance at 14 and in GCSEs showed that the most able (top 4%) did just as well in comprehensives as in grammar schools and that other able children actually did better at comprehensives. However, even as it was being reported, there were criticisms that Jesson ignored the value added by grammar schools between the ages of 11-14.

4
Discussion

This report began by noting recent and current developments in relation to possible ballots. Clearly, the coming months will be crucial in terms of deciding the future of grammar schools. Though they are now small in number, their existence continues to be prized by many. It has been noted that a majority of LEAs abolished selection in favour of comprehensive schools during the 1960s and 1970s. This was mostly in response to the development of new thinking about the reliability of and justifications for the 11-plus examination. In contrast to the national trend, several LEAs were not persuaded by the arguments in favour of fully comprehensive reorganization. In the face of considerable pressure for change during the 1970s a number of authorities managed to preserve at least one grammar school. Others retained a very high proportion of their selective schools.

Most of the remaining grammar schools are over-subscribed and, not surprisingly in view of the competition for places, most continue to have impressive academic records. Whether they are as impressive as they should be is an issue of concern, however. David Normington, head of the DfEE Schools Directorate, has suggested that a number of grammar schools were 'coasting at a level just high enough to keep them out of trouble' (Hattersley, 1998). In particular, he has questioned why any English grammar school should have less than 90% of its pupils gaining five or more A*-C GCSE grades (*TES*, 30 October 1998).

Nevertheless, the desirability of getting a grammar school education is evident in the many newspaper articles that highlight how parents move house to be in the 'right' catchment area and how this then causes localized house price inflation (for example *Daily Telegraph*, 14 September 1996 and 26 February 1999). However, critics argue that the grammar schools cream off bright children, handicapping other local schools. Moreover, while it is often claimed that grammar schools provide ladders of opportunity for bright working-class children, government figures show that they have hardly any pupils from poor families. In some parts of the country less than 1 per cent of grammar school pupils are eligible for free school meals, the most commonly used indicator of poverty. The figures came in a parliamentary answer showing less than 1 per cent of grammar school pupils on free meals in Stoke-on-Trent, Wiltshire and Shropshire, and less than 2 per cent in North Yorkshire, Buckinghamshire, Warwickshire and the London boroughs of Barnet, Bromley and Sutton. The grammar school average is 3.4 per cent, compared to a national average of 18 per cent (*The Guardian* 29 May 1999). Hattersley has written:

> The most absurd defence of selection is the pretence that it helps
> talented working-class boys and girls escape from the inner cities...
> The leg-up argument is simply not true. Selective schools remain in
> general beyond the reach of the lowest income groups. (Hattersley,
> 1998)

It cannot be assumed that the quality of debate during the coming months will be high or considered. The battle of information - and misinformation - relating to the possible implications of grammar school ballots has already begun. Kent County Council has recently claimed that the abolition of its 33 grammar schools could cost as much as £150 million, while Conservative Education spokesperson, Damian Green, forecast that the closure of all the remaining grammar schools would cost half a billion pounds (*BBC News Online*, 22 January 1999). A telephone survey of a majority sample of LEAs with grammar schools in January 1999 revealed, however, that no authority other than Kent firmly predicted additional costs. Its neighbouring authority, Medway, reported that there would be no extra expense and that there could be possible savings in having a fully comprehensive system. Buckinghamshire predicted some initial costs associated with the possible closure of its 13 grammar schools but did not anticipate an expensive upheaval (*BBC News Online*, 22 January 1999). Trafford LEA, which maintains seven grammar schools, might make annual savings based on test material and officer time of £250,000 (*TES*, 15 January 1999). Whether reorganization is seen as economic is likely to depend on the time scale being considered. It may well be that the high immediate cost of any reorganization would be balanced by the initially lower but longer term cost of retaining selection.

Whether these costs are considered worthwhile will depend on how one stands in relation to the educational costs of retaining or abandoning academic selection. Section Three of this report surveyed the most significant research contributions to the debates concerning selective and comprehensive education. If one were looking for clear-cut answers, the contributions are disappointing.

One point that has become clear as a result of undertaking this review is that selection is less politically contentious than was the case even ten years ago. It is interesting to note that a number of influential journalists who might at one time have been expected to be supporters of comprehensive education, including Will Hutton (*The Observer*), Melanie Phillips (*Sunday Times*) and Stephen Pollard (*The Express*), have regularly spoken and written in support of secondary school selection.

The present government, meanwhile, supports selection by aptitude, though not by ability. The confusing nomenclature and procedures to be found elsewhere in the state secondary school sector mirror the ambiguity of this policy. For example, neither Watford Grammar School for Boys nor Watford Grammar School for Girls will be subject to parental ballots, because they are officially classified as comprehensive schools. A glance at the former school's website http:// atschool.eduweb.co.uk/wbgs/prospectiveparents/admissions.html nevertheless reveals that its 'over subscription' criteria for Year Seven entry in 1999 include 'selection by academic *ability* (authors' emphasis) as measured by the school's assessment procedures, in merit order, for not more than 50 per cent of the places' (see also *Daily Telegraph*, 13 June 1998). It has been suggested that the practice of setting tests for Year Six pupils is increasingly being adopted by over-subscribed secondary schools. The trend is particularly strong among some of London's Church schools (*The Guardian*, 6 July 1999). Complaints about the selective practices of these and other secondary schools may now be referred to the Office of the School Adjudicator, headed by Sir Peter Newsam, a former Education Officer of the Inner London Education Authority and Director of the Institute of Education, University of London . The distinction between aptitude and ability is not convincing, even to expert educationists working in this field (see, for example, Edwards and Whitty, 1997; Edwards, 1998). According to Lord McIntosh of Haringey, the Deputy Chief Whip in the Upper House, however, it is unproblematic:

The Government have a very clear view of the difference involved: the difference is that as regards aptitude, which is applied to very specific specialisms – for example, modern languages, the performing arts, the visual arts, physical education, sport, design, technology and information technology – we could identify potential capacities to succeed. But that is very much not dependent on prior or current education achievement. (Hansard H. of L., 30 June 1999, col. 361)

Finally, it may be useful to consider some possible scenarios in the event of grammar school ballots being triggered during the coming months. A ballot favouring the status quo would resolve the present uncertainty relating to the future of the grammar schools in a particular area – at least for the next five years. Although this may at first sight look the 'easiest' of the scenarios, it may well present LEAs with a number of challenges. As LEAs and schools are required to set and meet ever more demanding performance targets, they may well find it difficult to address any polarization of attainment and the concentration of low-achieving pupils associated with selective systems of education. There are also suggestions that academic selection might have knock-on effects below and above the secondary phase. For instance, concentrating on grammar school entrance tests may suppress performance at Key Stage 2 and might also lead to low post-16 progression rates (Crook, Power and Whitty, 1999). The extent of this problem is likely to depend on many factors – not least the number of grammar schools in an area. Where an area is entirely selective, there is likely to be only limited scope for improvement. Some LEAs and governors may consider other initiatives, such as whether any secondary modern schools would benefit from seeking specialist school status. Such benefits might diminish if all schools took this route, however. A successful bid for an Education Action Zone could also be a mechanism for change, although it would be likely to involve only a small number of secondary schools. In terms of redressing the polarisation in performance more generally, it may be worth trying to address funding differences arising from provision for post-16 education. As Kerckhoff, Fogelman, Crook and Reeder (1996) point out, it may be that many of the differences in attainment between types of school are connected with resource allocation. Other differences, for instance, teacher attrition rates, may also merit attention.

In the event of a ballot favouring the abolition of the grammar school(s), the LEA would face a number of challenges. Indeed, critics claim that change will lead to chaos. It is argued, for instance, that many grammar schools are too small to become comprehensive and would have to close or merge. In addition to having to make reorganization proposals, the LEA may need to prepare for the possibility of any grammar school with a pre-twentieth century foundation leaving the maintained sector in favour of independent status. Late in 1998 the five King Edward Foundation schools in Birmingham indicated that they could become fee-paying independent schools; without them the state sector presence in the 'A' level top 40 would be halved. The foundation, set up in the 1550s, warned in November (*Financial Times*, 18 November 1998) that it would prefer to take this route. In the 1970s the foundation ran two direct grant schools which are now fully independent (*Financial Times*, 1 December 1998). But in the last resort the Secretary of State could stop a school closing down – a necessary precursor for any school wishing to go independent (*Financial Times*, 18 November 1998). A recent *Sunday Times* article suggested that more than a dozen grammar schools were making contingency plans to join the independent sector, including 870-year old Reading School and the Judd School in Kent. So too were Colchester Royal Grammar School which dates from the thirteenth century and Skegness School which dates from the fifteenth century. A further 11 in Kent, Bucks, North Yorkshire, Kingston upon Thames, Birmingham and Stratford-upon-Avon said they would consider going private. A number have substantial endowments so could charge competitive fees (*Sunday Times*, 4 July 1999). The move would recall developments in the 1970s when direct grant grammar schools became fee-paying to avoid becoming comprehensives.

LEAs might also discover that a number of parents opt in future to use the independent education sector, or possibly a grammar school in a neighbouring area where selective education has been retained. On the other hand, those parents opposed to selection who have had to look elsewhere for their children's secondary education in the past may well be drawn back into local maintained schools. An important factor in retaining parents within a comprehensive system after academic selection will be the extent to which the authority can reassure parents that the academically able will be equally well catered for within an all-ability school. To some extent this has been achieved elsewhere through various 'setting' and 'fast-tracking' arrangements – although these may often simply reproduce existing levels of polarization *within* rather than between schools. Some areas may be able to avail themselves of the extra support offered within the *Excellence in Cities* initiative.

Whichever strategies are put in place, LEAs will need to remember that developing successful comprehensive education will involve more than changing school names and reorganising buildings. It is likely to require a broader cultural shift if anxious parents, pupils and teachers – not to mention the media – are to be persuaded that comprehensive schools can provide as good an education as grammar schools

Yet, at a time when evidence-based policy is fashionable, it has to be said that the research evidence provides neither fuel for their fears nor succour for those who seek to persuade them that their fears are unfounded. Given the lack of clear evidence and the level of contention, it is perhaps not surprising that the Government has delegated the decision over the future of the grammar schools to parents. Whether this is the most sensible option in the long term remains to be seen.

APPENDIX A:
LIST OF SCHOOLS SUBJECT TO POSSIBLE BALLOTS

LEAs (and grammar schools) subject to a possible area ballot

LEA	Schools
Bexley	Bexley Grammar School
	Bexley-Erith Technical High School for Boys
	Chislehurst and Sidcup Grammar School
	Townley Grammar School for Girls
Buckinghamshire	Aylesbury Grammar School
	Aylesbury High School
	Beaconsfield High School
	Burnham Grammar School
	Chesham High School
	Dr Challoner's Grammar School
	Dr Challoner's High School
	John Hampden Grammar School
	Royal Grammar School
	Sir Henry Floyd Grammar School
	Sir William Borlase's Grammar School
	The Royal Latin School
	Wycombe High School
Kent	Barton Court Grammar School
	Borden Grammar School
	Chatham House Grammar School for Boys
	Clarendon House Grammar School
	Cranbrook School
	Dane Court Grammar School

Dartford Grammar School
Dartford Grammar School for Girls
Dover Grammar School for Boys
Dover Grammar School for Girls
Gravesend Grammar School for Boys
Gravesend Grammar School for Girls
Highsted School
Highworth Grammar School for Girls
Invicta Grammar School
Maidstone Grammar School
Maidstone Grammar School for Girls
Oakwood Park Grammar School
Queen Elizabeth's Grammar School
Simon Langton Girls' School
Simon Langton Grammar School for Boys
Sir Roger Manwood's School
The Folkestone School for Girls
The Grammar School for Girls
Wilmington
The Harvey Grammar School
The Judd School
The Norton Knatchbull School
The Skinners' School
Tonbridge Grammar School for Girls
Tunbridge Wells Girls' Grammar School
Tunbridge Wells Grammar School for Boys
Weald of Kent Grammar School
Wilmington Grammar School for Boys

Lincolnshire

Boston Grammar School
Boston High School for Girls
Bourne Grammar School

Caistor Grammar School
Carre's Grammar School
Kesteven and Grantham Girls' School
Kesteven and Sleaford High School
King Edward VI School
Queen Elizabeth's GM Grammar School
Queen Elizabeth's Grammar School
Horncastle
Queen Elizabeth's High School
Skegness Grammar School
Spalding Queen Elizabeth Royal Free
Grammar School
Spalding High School
The King's School

Medway

Chatham Boys' Grammar School
Chatham Girls' Grammar School
Fort Pitt Grammar School
Rainham Mark Grammar School
Sir Joseph Williamson's Mathematical
School
The Rochester Girls' Grammar School

Slough

Herschel Grammar School
Langley Grammar School
Slough Grammar School
St Bernard's Convent School

Southend

Southend High School for Boys
Southend High School for Girls
Westcliff High School for Boys
Westcliff High School for Girls

Surrey	Nonsuch High School for Girls
Sutton	Sutton Grammar School for Boys
	Wallington County Grammar School
	Wallington High School for Girls
	Wilson's School
Torbay	Churston Grammar School
	Torquay Boys' Grammar School
	Torquay Grammar School for Girls
Trafford	Altrincham Grammar School for Girls
	Altrincham Grammar School for Boys
	Loreto Grammar School
	Sale Grammar School
	St Ambrose College
	Stretford Grammar School
	Urmston Grammar School

Groups of grammar schools subject to a possible ballot

LEA area	*Groups of Grammar Schools*
Barnet	Queen Elizabeth's School
	St Michael's Catholic Grammar School
	The Henrietta Barnett School
Birmingham	Bishop Vesey's Grammar School
	Handsworth Grammar School
	King Edward VI Aston School
	King Edward VI Camp Hill Girls' School
	King Edward VI Camp Hill School (Boys)
	King Edward VI Five Ways School

	King Edward VI Handsworth School
	Sutton Coldfield Girls' School
Bournemouth	Bournemouth School
	Bournemouth School for Girls (GM)
Bromley	Newstead Woods School for Girls (GM)
	St Olave's and St Saviour's Grammar School
Calderdale	Crossley Heath School
	The North Halifax Grammar School
Essex	Chelmsford County High School for Girls
	Colchester County High School for Girls
	Colchester Royal Grammar School
	King Edward VI Grammar School (GM)
Gloucestershire	High School for Girls
	Marling School
	Ribston Hall High School
	Sir Thomas Rich's School
	Stroud High School
	The Crypt School
Lancashire	Lancaster Girls' Grammar School
	Lancaster Royal Grammar School
Kingston-upon-Thames	The Tiffin Girls' School
	Tiffin School
North Yorkshire	Ermysted's Grammar School
	Skipton Girls' High School

Plymouth	Devonport High School for Boys
	Devonport High School for Girls
	Plymouth High School for Girls
Poole	Parkstone Grammar School (Girls)
	Poole Grammar School
Reading	Kendrick Girls' Grammar School
	Reading School
Redbridge	Ilford County High School
	Woodford County High School
Walsall	Queen Mary's Grammar School
	Queen Mary's High School
Warwickshire	King Edward VI Grammar School
	Lawrence Sheriff School
	Rugby High School for Girls
	Stratford-Upon-Avon Grammar School for Girls
Wiltshire	Bishop Wordsworth's Grammar School
	South Wilts Grammar School for Girls
Wirral	Calday Grange Grammar School
	St Anselm's College
	Upton Hall Convent School FCJ
	West Kirby Grammar School for Girls
	Wirral County Grammar School (Girls)
	Wirral Grammar School for Boys
The Wrekin	Adams' Grammar School
	Newport Girls' High School

Stand Alone Grammar Schools

LEA area	Grammar school
Cumbria	Queen Elizabeth Grammar School
Devon	Colyton Grammar School
Enfield	The Latymer School
Gloucestershire	Pate's Grammar School
Kirklees	Heckmondwike Grammar School
Lancashire	Bacup and Rawtenstall Grammar School Clitheroe Royal Grammar School
Liverpool	The Liverpool Blue Coat School
North Yorkshire	Ripon Grammar School
Stoke on Trent	St Joseph's College
Warwickshire	Alcester Grammar School
Wolverhampton	Wolverhampton Girls' High School

APPENDIX B

Meaning of 'eligible parent'

4. (1) ... in relation to an area ballot or a petition for such a ballot a person is an 'eligible parent' on any date if –

(a) on that date the person is a registered parent of a child who is a registered pupil at school –

  (i) maintained by the local education authority for the relevant area in question ...

(b) on that date the person is resident in the relevant area in question and is a registered parent of a child who is a registered pupil at an independent school situated in the area; or

(c) on that date the person is a parent who does not fall within sub-paragraph (a) or (b), is resident in the relevant area in question and is the parent of a child who –

  (i) is a pupil at a school (whether it is maintained by a local education authority, a special school not maintained by a local education authority or an independent school), or

  (ii) is being educated otherwise than at school, or

  (iii) has not begun to be of compulsory school age,

and who is registered with the designated body ...

BIBLIOGRAPHY

Adonis, A. and Pollard, S. (1997), *A Class Act: The Myth of Britain's Classless Society.* London: Hamish Hamilton.

Baldwin, R.W. (1975), *The Great Comprehensive Gamble.* Manchester: Helios Press.

Ball, S. (1981), *Beachside Comprehensive: A Case Study of Secondary Schooling.* Cambridge: Cambridge University Press.

Ball, S. (ed.) (1984), *Comprehensive Schooling: A Reader.* London: Falmer.

Barber, M. (1994), *The Making of the 1944 Education Act.* London: Cassell.

Barker, B. (1986), *Rescuing the Comprehensive Experience.* Milton Keynes: Open University Press.

Benn, C. (annually 1967-72), *Comprehensive Reorganization in Britain.* London: Comprehensive Schools Committee.

Benn, C. (1992), 'Common education and the radical tradition' in A. Rattansi and D. Reeder (eds), *Rethinking Radical Education: Essays in Honour of Brian Simon.* London: Lawrence and Wishart, pp.142-165.

Benn, C. and Simon, B. (1970), *Half Way There: Report on the British Comprehensive School Reform.* London: McGraw-Hill. (Second edition published in 1972 by Penguin).

Benn, C. and Chitty, C. (1996), *Thirty Years On: Is Comprehensive Education Alive and Well or Struggling to Survive?* London: David Fulton.

Brock, C. (1995), *Rutlish School: The First Hundred Years.* London: Rutlish School.

Burgess, R.G. (1983), *Experiencing Comprehensive Education: A Study of Bishop McGregor School.* London: Methuen.

Chitty, C. (ed.) (1987). *Redefining the Comprehensive Experience.* London: Institute of Education.

— (1989), *Towards a New Education System: The Victory of the New Right?* London: Falmer.

— (1994), 'Thirty Years On', *Forum* 36, 3:89-90.

Clifford, P. and Heath, A. (1984), 'Selection does make a difference', *Oxford Review of Education* 10, 1:85-97.

Cox, B. and Dyson, A. (eds.) (1969a), *Fight for Education: A Black Paper.* London: Critical Quarterly Society.

– (eds.) (1969b), *Black Paper Two: The Crisis in Education.* London: Critical Quarterly Society.

Cox, C. and Marks, J. (1980), *Real Concern: An Appraisal of the National Children's Bureau Report on Progress in Secondary Schools.* London: Centre for Policy Studies.

– (1988), *The Insolence of Office: Education and the Civil Servants.* London: Claridge Press.

Crook, D. (1993), 'Edward Boyle: Conservative champion of comprehensives?', *History of Education* 22, 1:49-62.

Crook, D., Power. S. and Whitty, G. (1999) *Review of Research Evidence into Selective and Comprehensive Education for Medway Council,* London: Institute of Education, University of London.

Dale, R.R. and Griffith, S. (1965), *Down Stream: Failure in the Grammar School.* London: Routledge and Kegan Paul.

Department for Education (1992), *Choice and Diversity: A New Framework for Schools* (White Paper Cmnd. 2021). London: HMSO.

Department of Education and Science (1965), *The Organization of Secondary Education* (Circular 10/65). London: HMSO.

— (1978), *Comprehensive Education: Report of a DES Conference.* London: HMSO.

— (1983), 'School standards and spending: statistical analysis', *Statistical Bulletin* 16/83. DES: London.

— (1984), 'School standards and spending: Statistical analysis: A further appreciation', *Statistical Bulletin* 13/84. DES: London.

Douglas, J.W.B. (1964), *The Home and the School.* London: Macgibbon and Kee.

Duffield, J. (1998), 'Unequal opportunities, or don't mention the (class) war', unpublished paper presented to the Scottish Educational Research Association conference, available online at http://www.leeds.ac.uk/educol./documents/000000820.htm

Edwards, T. (1998) *Specialisation without Selection?* RISE Briefing No. 1, London: Research and Information on State Education Trust.

Edwards, T. and Whitty, G. (1997), 'Specialisation and selection in secondary education', *Oxford Review of Education* 23, 1:5-15.

Eysenck, H. (1991), 'Equality and education: fifteen years on', *Oxford Review of Education* 17:161-67.

Fearn, E. (1980), 'The local politics of comprehensive secondary reorganisation' in E. Fearn and B. Simon (eds), *Education in the 1960s.* Leicester: History of Education Society, pp.35-58.

— (1983), 'Comprehensive reorganisation: some priorities in research', *History of Education Society Bulletin* 32:43-50.

— (1989), 'The politics of local reorganisation' in R. Lowe (ed.), *The Changing Secondary School.* London: Routledge and Kegan Paul, pp.36-51.

Fenwick, I. (1976), *The Comprehensive School, 1944-70*. London: Methuen.

Fitz, J., Halpin, D. and Power, S. (1993), *Grant Maintained Schools: Education in the Market Place*. London: Kegan Page.

Floud, J., Halsey, A.H. and Martin, F.M. (1956), *Social Class and Educational Opportunity*. London: Heinemann.

Ford, J. (1969), *Social Class and the Comprehensive School*. London: Routledge and Kegan Paul.

Gray, J. and Jesson, D. (1989), 'The impact of comprehensive refoms' in R. Lowe (ed.), *The Changing Secondary School*. London: Falmer Press, pp.72-98.

Gray, J., Jesson, D. and Jones, B. (1984), 'Predicting differences in examination results between local education authorities: Does school organisation matter?', *Oxford Review of Education* 10, 1:69-74.

Gray, J., McPherson, A.F. and Raffe, D. (1983), *Reconstructions of Secondary Education*. London: Routledge and Kegan Paul.

Griggs, C. (1989), 'The new right and English secondary education' in R. Lowe (ed.), *The Changing Secondary School*. London: Falmer, pp.99-128.

Halsey, A.H. (1957), *Social Class and Educational Opportunity*. London: Heinemann.

— (1965), 'Education and equality', *New Society* 17, June, pp.13-15.

Halsey, A.H., Heath, A.F. and Ridge, J.M. (1980), *Origins and Destinations: Family, Class and Education in Modern Britain*. Oxford: Clarendon Press.

Hansard (1997), House of Commons written answer, 25 November, col.492.

Hargreaves, D.H. (1967), *Social Relations in a Secondary School*. London: Routledge and Kegan Paul.

Hattersley, R. (1998), 'Grammar power', *The Guardian*, 26 November.

Hillman, J. (1994), 'Education in Northern Ireland' in National Commission on Education, *Insights into Education and Training*. London: Heinemann, pp.361-401.

Jackson, B. and Marsden, D. (1962), *Education and the Working Class*. London: Routledge and Kegan Paul.

James, P.H. (1980), *The Reorganization of Secondary Education*. Slough: NFER.

Jarvis, F. (1993), *Education and Mr. Major: Correspondence Between the Prime Minister and Fred Jarvis*. London: Tufnell Press.

Judge, H. (1984), *A Generation of Schooling: English Secondary Schools since 1944*. Oxford: Oxford University Press.

Kent Education Committee (1974), *Education in Kent, 1968-74*. Maidstone: Kent Education Committee.

Kerckhoff, A.C. and Trott, J. (1993), 'Educational attainment in a changing educational system: the case of England and Wales' in Shavit and Blossfeld, *op. cit.*, pp.133-53.

Kerckhoff, A.C., Fogelman, K., Crook, D. and Reeder, D. (1996), *Going Comprehensive in England and Wales: A Study of Uneven Change*. London: Woburn Press.

Koshe, G. (1957), 'A comparative study of the attainments and intelligence of children in certain comprehensive, grammar and secondary modern schools', unpublished University of London MA thesis.

Lacey, C. (1970), *Hightown Grammar: The School as a Social System*. Manchester: Manchester University Press.

Lawton, D. (1975), *Class, Culture and the Curriculum*. London: Routledge and Kegan Paul.

Lee, A.M. (1999), *Private and State Provision in Education: Why such polarisation?* Windsor: St George's House.

London County Council (1961), *London Comprehensive Schools.* London: London County Council.

McPherson, A. and Raab, C. (1988), *Governing Education: A Sociology of Policy since 1945.* Edinburgh: Edinburgh University Press.

McPherson, A. and Willms, J.D. (1987), 'Equalisation and improvement: Some effects of comprehensive reorganisation in Scotland', *Sociology* 21:509-39.

Marks, J. (1991), *Standards in Schools: Assessment, Accountability and the Purposes of Education.* London: Social Market Foundation.

— (1998), *An Anatomy of Failure: Standards in English Schools for 1997.* London: Social Market Foundation.

Marks, J. and Pomian-Srzednicki, M. (1985), *Standards in English Schools: Second Report.* London: National Council for Educational Standards.

Marks, J., Cox, C. and Pomian-Srzednicki, M. (1983), *Standards in English Schools.* London: National Council for Educational Standards.

Marks, J. and Cox, C. (1984), 'Educational attainment in secondary schools', *Oxford Review of Education* 10, 1, pp.7-31.

Marks, J., Cox, C. and Pomian-Srzednicki, M. (1986), *Examination Performance of Secondary Schools in the Inner London Education Authority.* London: National Council for Educational Standards.

Monks, T.G. (1968), *Comprehensive Education in England and Wales: A Survey of Schools and their Organisation.* Slough: National Foundation for Educational Research.

Morris, M. and Griggs, C. (1988), 'Thirteen wasted years' in M. Morris and C. Griggs (eds), *Education: The Wasted Years? 1973-1986.* London: Falmer Press.

PERSPECTIVES ON EDUCATION POLICY

Moser, C. (1997), *Reforming Education in the United Kingdom: The Vital Priorities* (1996 Annual Sir Charles Carter Lecture). Belfast: Northern Ireland Economic Council.

National Commission on Education (1993), *Learning to Succeed: A Radical Look at Education Today and a Strategy for the Future.* London: Heinemann.

Newsam, P. (1996), 'Take the terminology to task', *Times Educational Supplement,* 22 March.

Palmer, A. (1998), *Schooling Comprehensive Kids: Pupil Responses to Education.* Aldershot: Ashgate.

Paterson, L. (1997), 'Individual autonomy and comprehensive education', *British Educational Research Journal* 23, 3:315-27.

Patten, J. (1992), 'Who's afraid of the "S" word?', *New Statesman and Society* 17, July, pp.20-21.

Pedley, R. (1963; 1969 2nd edition), *The Comprehensive School.* Harmondsworth: Penguin.

Pollard, S. (1995), *Schools, Selection and the Left.* London: Social Market Foundation.

Pring, R. and Walford, G. (eds) (1997), *Affirming the Comprehensive Ideal.* London: Falmer Press.

Reynolds, D. and Sullivan, M. with Murgatroyd, S. (1987), *The Comprehensive Experiment: A Comparison of the Selective and Non-Selective System of School Organisation.* London: Falmer Press.

Ringer, F. (1979), *Education and Society in Modern Europe.* Bloomington and London: Indiana University Press.

Rubinstein, D. and Simon, B. (1969), *The Evolution of the Comprehensive School, 1926-1966.* London: Routledge and Kegan Paul.

Shavit, Y. and Blossfeld, H-P. (1993) (eds), *Persistent Inequality: Changing Educational Attainment in Thirteen Countries.* Colorado and Oxford: Boulder, Co, Westview Press.

Silver, H. (1994), *Good Schools, Effective Schools: Judgements and their Histories*. London: Cassell.

Silver, H. and Silver, P. (1991), *An Educational War on Poverty: American and British Policy-Making, 1960-1980*. Cambridge: Cambridge University Press.

Simon, B. (1991), *Education and the Social Order, 1940-1990*. London: Lawrence and Wishart.

Steedman, J. (1980), *Progress in Secondary Schools*. London: National Children's Bureau.

Steedman, J. (1983), *Examination Results in Selective and Non-Selective Schools*. London: National Children's Bureau.

Steedman, J. (1987), 'Longitudinal survey research into progress in secondary schools, based on the National Child Development Study' in G. Walford (ed.), *Doing Sociology of Education*. London: Falmer Press, pp.177-206.

Steedman, J., K. Fogelman and D. Hutchison (1980), *Real Research*. London: National Children's Bureau.

Thane, P. (1982), *The Foundations of the Welfare State*. London: Longman.

Thatcher, M. (1995), *The Path to Power*. London: Harper Collins.

Vernon, P.E. (ed.) (1957), *Secondary School Selection*. London: Methuen.

Walford, G. (1994), 'A return to selection?', *Westminster Studies in Education* 17:19-30.

Yates, A. and Pidgeon, D.A. (1957), *Admission to Grammar Schools*. London: NFER.